salt//water

william t marshe

NeoPoiesisPress.com

ℛ

NeoPoiesis Press, LLC

2775 Harbor Ave SW, Suite D, Seattle, WA 98126-2138
Inquiries: Info@NeoPoiesisPress.com
NeoPoiesisPress.com

salt/ /water
ISBN 978-0-9903565-1-6 (pbk)

    1. Poetry. I. marshe, william.

Library of Congress Control Number: 2015912263

First Edition

Cover Artwork: Stephen Roxborough
Cover Design: Milo Duffin and Stephen Roxborough

Printed in the United States of America.

for U, all of U

Contents

water

salt

courage my love

fold and slip

thin lines

the apocalypse of reason

masses

water

picking cape breton blueberries

there is no cure for being island born,
and that infection burns in early morning hours
as the mind bends the back and climbs again
the steep hillside rising from the road,
the waters of the atlantic churning below.

the looming church rests, isolated in its watch,
but for the white marble faces of the ancient dead,
which are chewed by summer wind and winter ice;
little peace having come to their hearts
as they face, forever, that distant glasgow shore.

an empty tin pail swings, impatiently,
on the tether of a young man's reach.
the wild blueberries, ripe to giving, droop;
swollen by the teasing caress of the ocean's kiss.
they long to dance this sunday evening.

and these small blue eyes, rising from the ground,
are nearly three centuries deep and growing;
dressed by yawning water and a reflective sky.
in my misted memory, far above that ship-less sea,
there are two for the pail, and ten for me.

vous dancer?

i entrust my drifting feet
to a fiery cajun rhythm
and my ears to the staggering melody
of a drunken violin.
i give my heart to their explosive joy,
from the depths of my history in exile.

eyes shut and chin to chest,
i two step left and spin,
and spin, and spin.

i spin in the bosom of the bayou,
out across an aching land.
i spin into the arms
of that western isle royale shore.

let's wander home, mez amee,
to a setting cheticamp sun
and a kissing petit etange breeze.

spin with me into the salty night.
twirl with me at a cod and halibut fete.
dance in the ballroom of a balladeer whale,
and sail her belle fontaine into a timeless air.

she

she is the stone
rippling waters,
shattering the glass,
splitting the skin
and breaking the bones.

she is the tripping,
the hard ground coming,
pain and its time,
the off balance,
affliction's simple song.

she is the zero
of nothing owing,
nothing to receive,
the empty hand,
the barren field.

monarch

her body
is a major journey

her heart a constellation
shifting to the blue

her skin
accepts the pulses
of anticipation

> a door
> accepts the knock

hands open
an arm believes
itself the wind

inside a seed
our flower hopes to bloom

spring knocks
on a tightly wrapped cocoon
until hearts flutter.

come

unbelievable miles
storyteller mystic
saviour and witness
foretelling the sun

lay silken silence
on this flower's bed

come
to cause a stirring

> knock
> to have the door open

lake ontario

i treated you poorly all
those moments when
comparisons were a way
of dealing with sorrow   how
often we shared   then i drift
inland -give you little credit
  -defame you to others

you know so little of the
ocean you try to be ignoring
your gesture instead i laugh when
backs are turned   -pretend your
waves seem endless —pretend your
murky depths hide wonder
ful strange creatures —mocking
with my condescendence

we were never mated —souls
sitting on the same bench only
night after night   many nights
the ethereal kiss always escap
ing us   not your fault or mine
or theirs or ancestors
generations to come   -just a
fact and understood

i do love you   my   loss   not
your burden yet i expect at times
for you to take my weight and
i thank you —with sneers   yet
those quiet evenings when you
allowed me to watch a sun's
gentle strokes of your heaving
belly

two have made the best of
it –i learned to be held and
you learned to hold as i settled
blended my salt with
the absence of your's while
you came to know the long
distant swell crashing against
my shore –the ocean -you
so wish to be inside me
–raising a tide against my
heart

i do love you   -do recognize
your unconditional offers when
lying in my room   in winter miss
ing you when alone i come around
eventually i come around   –accept
you cannot be the forceful engine
driving my passions   but you
still give understanding   -arms

no wonder

i arrived
in this world
by the ocean.
it's no wonder
        salty water leads me home.
        the curling tears on your face.
        the still sweat on your breast.
        the warm ripple of passion
        between your thighs.

i arrived
in this world
one september.
it's no wonder
        autumn grips my love.
        the fading is sleep.
        the quiet before rebirth
        follows the thrill of release.

i arrived
in this world
in the depth of night.
it's no wonder
        when i close my eyes
        i see most clearly.
        when you turn on your light,
        i leave the room.
        i thrive in the corner
        of your darkest september.

cabot head, georgian bay

this landscape was crafted
for painters and photographers,
but to me, the passionate lover,

strolling the smooth stones
at the edge of the deep, clear water
of georgian bay,

lacking the savory smell
of beached urchins and weeds;
of angel hair tumbling in cresting waves;

it is a two dimensional facsimile.
it is the touch of a heartless lover,
looking away

at the exact moment
you start believing
movement can become
meaning.

shadow woods

when, again, will you dance with me,
into that shadow woods;
to lift our voices with the beetle's and the centipede's;
to whisper confidences to Robin's witches;
to lie on the warm, damp skin of decay,
staring at the floor of heaven above?

i am waiting; so silently waiting.
my pocketed hands fumbling with keys.
the broken green of the canopy
leaks sun into my vision,

and at the fringe of this silence,
forty-four fragments of night take flight.
a chorus of widow birds sing a plea to me,

> *'come, come;*
>   *she is here.*
> *follow, follow;*
>   *she sees you.'*

i lunge toward the sky with my featherless hopes.
i run out of the bracken and feign to fly,
but the tired wind has lost its will to carry fools.

i've run into a barren land,
too near to cryptic roads and heavy gravity.

i'll make this easy…
the wind taken from me, i sit down.

the pall bearers of poems
can take, from here, longing.
it is finished.
take only longing.

she will take the rest
to carry in her satchel breast.

this limp body of language
she will tuck in with the beetles
between the roots of giants

or dip it to dissolve in the silky silt
of a clear and honest brook

or bear it to her sea,
to bury deep beneath the ivory glow
of that ancient midden shore of shells.

she will sing me witch's songs,
about our shadow woods.

she binds herself to rain

she binds herself

   to driftwood,
the failing shade of bone;

   to the affection
of alder smoke and cedar bows;

   to the poorest
in a nation of knots, near a sweater's tear;

   to any uneven hour
and it's awkward extra
     chime;

   to the frost
caressing a useless window pane

  too old for clarity.
  so cracked, too cracked
  to fend against the draft
  on her shivering skin.

she binds herself

   to a timid shadow,
like a bird, yet unbound from its stone gray shell

she binds herself

   to the feather
of a lullaby's sweetest refrain,

played by a late evening rain.

to the dance (a glosa)

But we grow old! Ah! When shall all men's good
Be each man's rule, and universal peace
Lie like a shaft of light across the land,
And like a lane of beams athwart the sea

The Golden Year, Alfred Lord Tennyson

to the dance

Memory wears his sunday best;
so slick his hair, so straight his back.
his sister, Time, is in a gown of mist.
his brother, Loss, tightens his grip
around his sister's, Love's, dainty wrist.
they sashay through the greening woods,
on their way to church, or perhaps a dance.
so ripe with youth. so right with hope.
so tall with promise, being all they could,
But we grow old! Ah! When shall all men's good?

two handsome young men, in their shining year,
Memory and Loss: their fates tilled but unsown,
stand proud near the sides of Time and Love;
tilting heads for the strangers, smiling for the known.
they'll scuff the shine off their sunday shoes,
on rough country roads and hard city streets.
they'll soil the cuff of their hard pressed slacks.
the cost of joy: a few specks of dust.
so, to own one's life, and not to lease,
Be each man's rule, and universal peace.

such lovely young ladies! Such rhyming flowers!
Time and Love in their white, white hour.
they will, in their way, in their moment,
come to heal the sick, come to brighten a day.
they're the older of the four, and gentler by years
than their reckless brothers with their dirty hands.
they glow like the summer. they nourish like rain.
they're faith in the winter that a night never lasts.
they move like an ocean shifting the sand;
Lie like a shaft of light across the land

they grew old. ah. they grew old.
a family such as this, with ties that bind
well beyond the grave, could twirl in youth
but knew they must age, must learn to behave.
they grew old. joints stiffened with pain.
Memory, Time, Love and Loss would be
the slant of a sunset, the corner of an eye,
the shift in a landscape, the drift in the snow,
the way the day breaks between the trees,
And like a lane of beams athwart the sea.

fresh water

i'm balancing in the middle
of a clear, determined river,
listening to its ageless song.

i'm standing, knee deep,
in a north river's cold water
on slippery, granite boulders,
waiting with the rainbow trout
and speckled frogs.

i'd lie down in that river,
to be baptised into the faith
of its carelessness;

its healing hands
smoothing the scars;
washing the skin clean
from the sticky residue of loss.

carry away
the limp memories
of fishing with a father gone.

leave me as a fresh water fish
in the deeper pools,
where water falls;

where the limbs
of october trees
point over head;
point to a larger sky;
point to a distance.

end of a pier

the boards are rough
and lifting,
their edges rotting.

a bridge to grain carriers
        coal carriers
        passenger liners
        steam, sail, and diesel
        drifting

a bridge with one foot on land,
        one foot dangling
        in the silent harbour.

a bridge to open waters

waves echo
the last rhythmic steps
which danced
across its willing support.

were they heading shore side?
were they marching toward
the wet horizon, to never return?
is this why these weak boards wait?
were there promises made?

angle wings

the clouds are easy targets.
they make little or no effort
to dodge the gauge of my 20.20 eyes.
so flamboyant in their fluffy stoles.
reflecting vivid hues, night or noon,
they walk over us all.

never a miserly dollar held back.
their surplus tossed about, with abandon.
huge, they are, beside the airbus soaring.
so small, against the tree, i hide beneath.
i steal their identity daily.
they never miss it.

the rain drops, their rain drops,
in droves. they come hammering.
uncountable numbers of boisterous revellers.

i could swallow them, one by one. like i,
the coming sun sees through their guise.
one by one, they are gathered and returned.

the random few will try and hide,
sneaking beneath the cellar and the stone,
but our roots are deeper still
and one H or two, perhaps an Oh,
the earth, as well, will send them packing.

(these rain beasts, rain villains, rain pomposity)
they seek to trap us in our homes, to flood us out
like that innocent snail,
driven from the garden to the stoop,
its hard shell strong against the beetle,
but an upside down bowl: no place to be
when the ocean is on the move.
to higher ground! scale the wall!

it moved as quick as it could.
it tried and gave its all,
but hardly stood a chance beneath my blind foot;
the crunch of my reckless abandon coming down.
it is like this.

it was raining equally on both of us
and fate would have it, not i,
but I
was larger, stronger, faster.
my head being closer to the bosom of the clouds,
i did not see it coming.

i carry on beyond this,
passed my fallen comrade,
ever forward and down,
like the sand, the hapless sand,
in the path of the river
(the river of now, not forever).

each magnificent granule swept away,
being a part of the path of least resistance.
some go wailing, not wanting to leave
the tender arms of their retaining wall.
swept, profoundly, away.
tiny aboriginals
against the drive of a moving civilization,
a marching history making its way,
the canyon in its infancy,
the broom, the broom of Neruda's death.

others went willingly, glad for the change,
kin to Heraclitus,
appreciative of the ride,
moving with the tide,
the changing landscape,
their destinations un-cemented.
flow on, mighty stream, flow on!

soon, this benevolent catastrophe will end.
the goods i've stolen will nourish the daisies,
the lavender and the stinkweed, equally.

i'll quit this radical life;
lay down this activist vision;
fail this mutinous up rising.
i will walk the path of least resistance.

in a dream of the aftermath,
a blanket of black flies
spreads before me.
i pass through with little effort.
they are sucked into my lungs.
they're breathed one by one.
they swim in the saliva lake of my mouth.
they tangle in the sweaty hairs
of my naked, out stretched arms.

they dance about, each one
an ever changing camera angle
on my position.

i borrow a billion tiny eyes from
the bodies of quantum angles with wings.
i become a cloud buster.
i become their airbus.
i become a pool of night.

beneath the heavy boot of nature's reckless abandon,
i become the snail.

cucumber

the potatoes are underground.
it's impossible to know
if they are growing or
how many there are.
have they rotted from too much water?
are they even potatoes?

and the tomato:
(forward thinking, difficult)
i'd have to return to it
to see how a heart can hang
in the open air and accumulate
dew through the long cool night
and flush itself to fullness,
daily.

daily
hanging from its vine,
deeply red and sharply shadowed;
a heart: plumb, and swollen
with the evening sun.

i come to the cucumber,
long and thick beneath the leaf
canopy it has built for itself.

it's about the cucumber.

it has always been
about the cucumber.

tree

how can i say tree and be certain
you understand the tree i'm speaking of,
when i fail nailing that tree down myself?

have i said elm: with its ability to swim against any wave?

or willow: so swift and able to bend with any wind?

or spruce: modestly said and fragrant in the cool evening air?

or giant redwood: above all others; cloud kisser and king?

do i mean a tree, green
in the dancing light of morning?
or brown, in the hollow sleep of winter?

the brittle ficus? the thin juniper?

and is that tree closer to sapling or floorboard?

there were many trees around in my youth.
not a forest, exactly, times being what they were
but we were able to afford enough.
i never imagine it would be so easy
to walk out of that wood.

at times i recall a large maple, in wentworth park,
where, in late september, i would sit
to watch the ducks waddling by,
reposed on a wide blanket of fallen yellow leaves;
a magic carpet of leisure.

it's not that one.

do i mean the silent trees on the edge of the forchu highway,
rendered feeble by the fire of '79; bones in an endless field
of bones, but, appearing as if they had nearly escaped?

Pablo, our dear Pablo, could wander into any room
and whisper something like
        esto es el arbol;
then half a nation would sway and that whisper would echo
through empty souls for generations.
        el arbol... el arbol...

perhaps i'm meant to wait until enough others have said tree to me,
then, work like a 19th century gear and replicate, as close as possible,

a most elegant tree. a most sincere tree. a most delicate tree.

and pray it's not hollowed out by weevils
before it blooms.

i say tree, sometimes, and i feel you believe i mean tangible,
brute and raw entwined branches in a dense wood

or that useless tree, blocking the sun in our yard. An axe! An axe
to that bastard and down he'll go! Shade! i've no use for shade!

again, and again.

that is not what i meant, at all. that is not it at all.

again and again, i can do nothing.

i am only the sawyer of tree
and you,
you are the hearer of tree.

it's in your hands.

everything is in your hands.

far inland

i exist far inland, now,
with hard surfaces and
sharp reflections of nothing.
the music here is harsh...
hard to measure in certain terms.
the cold here is not Romantic.
it doesn't bring ideas
of fireplaces and hot drinks,
nor wool covers and
the arms of a lover.

it's just cold.

to know me, now,
is to know loss, to know smog,
overcrowded, overbuilt, overpass.

to know me is to know sorrow...
disjointed, walking endlessly,
looking, feeling, sniffing
like a starving raccoon in a trash can,
searching for some small thing,
to bring back a memory of
who i was.

they've even taken that.

when i sit on my top step at night
with cigarette smoke filling my lungs
        (as if smoke could fill a void)
i squint to see if i can catch
a glimpse of the lake:
my false sea and when seeing it,
it only serves to break me more.

jellyfish

we dangled off the edge of a wharf
on the edge of the new world
edging into morning
into each other

between closed mouths
and eye blinks
we threatened each other
with success, with
i will leave this place
i'll not forget you

      out all night, the sun meandered home
      poking its slow way
      through the clear harbour water
      and the bodies
      of a million jellyfish

      which came in with the tide
      and would leave with the same

a million missed tides later
i have not forgotten them

night shift

the fountain slows.
the water of its day waning,
till it sleeps.

a wicker chair curls
against a table whose
thin skin is wrapped
in a moss sweater.

they, too, sleep.

now, the furnace grunts
and curses aching muscles,
ceased too long. it lunges
awake, feeling once again, vital.

there are long nights coming.

some will sleep.

others work, as on any night
(the cooler night, the warm night,
the dry, the humid, the icy or wet
night)

some will sleep
and others work;

each, in their turn,
knowing their moment.

unwelcome in the garden

the thin shadows of leaf less trees
stretch across unblemished snow.
a buried sundial peeks, timeless,
into the cold.

i disturb the garden's affairs,
my eyes digging a path into the forest,
to a forsaken brook no longer babbling
about the frivolity of summer's days.

a goose squats on a frozen pond;
a squirrel on a hollow stump,
as i climb an icy slope.

water less falls.
silent, sleeping stones.
everything smoothing the quiet;
this garden's sanctioned respite from:

> *The children, The dogs, The lovers, The unhappy,*
> *The discontented, The lonely, The inspired, The thief,*
> *The breakers, The diggers, The polluters, The old,*
> *The young, The middle aged, The stray cat, The skunks,*
> *The truant, The lost, The forgiven, The singer,*
> *The song, The birds, The weeds, The leaves,*
> *The hot dry earth, The beer bottle, The journalist,*
> *The singular, The determined, The gardener, The runner,*
> *The subtle, The sick, The prince, The harbinger and*

me.

my footsteps crack the outer layer;
breaking through the whispered prayers
i was never meant to hear.

un-greened

the world has un-greened itself.
i see the brown bark beneath the leaf.
i see the black soil under the grass.
i see the dull worm mixing that soil,
writhing in its sepia tones.

the world, in its screaming
through the long night
has developed a rasp in its voice.
now, unable to reach, effectively,
the falsetto of a rising sun
it only hums in baser notes.

this is the uplifting part.
i'm skipping the stanza about *her*,
leaving her leased part of the page
blank.

i speak of winter in july
and wonder about the growing
funereal lament of a summer
which has stopped trying.

leslie street spit

these thin, frozen, puddles are literal.
those heavy, random, stones are literal.
the grey, stripped bare, branches are literal.
thirty eight thousand or more cormorants,
huddled, are literal.

i am the only figurative body here,
yet i feel this literal wind
on my foolishly metaphorical skin.

my neck compacts
so the lobes of my ears
are below the upturned collar
of my black wool jacket.
i walk with fleecy feet.

these birds are a squatting nation.
there are gangs near a brick pile,
and a few on the twisted rebar.
seventeen or more
on the breakwater boulders,

and the trees seem to wear them
as december leaves;
as night leaves;
as an animated, downy coat of leaves;
as leaves;
as literal leaves.

squawks and cracking ice echoes.
there is sunshine in the chill.
they swallow it into their blackness.
i swallow it into my shiver.

with each soiling foot fall,
i am more and more among them.
a crooked ugly bird on
reclaimed lands of feather,
filth and broken buildings.

prophets in the mud

1979, Newfoundland...2010, Gulf of Mexico

is it too late for surrender?

as a boy i stand
on the belly of a pilot whale,
a hundred or more
stretching the shore
of point au gaul.

these shards of night carried in
by the slow, cold hands of the atlantic.

billowing black sheets of sorrow.
were they crying to the deaf
or had they simply resolved 'it's not worth it',
and come to lie their heaviness down
on this shore of darkness?

there is as much opportunity
for failure
as there is for success.
both come.

and the blood of black death
dances on the surf
again.

the dark liquid of ingenuity
washes feathers and scales
and seeps deep into
the shells and the sand.

a pungent ink
is scrawling damnations
on the backs of the innocent.

*yet, it's one small stitch
in a growing fabric of capability.*

we're as blameless in this
as are the bizarre choices of nature.

mitigate losses: move on.

is it too late to throw arms in the air?
do we march toward the beach
and lie down?
do we let our children console themselves
with the belief we're merely resting
and soon we'll swim
back out to sea?

get in the car. go home.
the whales have finished singing.

there is a shadow
crawling the length of our shore.

shipwreck, big tub, tobermory

The Schooner 'Sweepstakes'

what hope could anyone expect
from a vessel christened 'chance'?

she was weighed low, from her birth,
with a heavy cargo of irony.

her hull: a forest carved
to an unnatural precision

of angles and flowing arcs,
shaped from a lifeless heartwood.

they burdened her belly with bushels of wheat
then set her to sail their dried brown field

over the rolling waves of huron's bay,
into the lap of the unkempt knave.

they hung, over her arms, clouds of white,
thinking her able to harness the wind

but, instead, the wind, not one for restraint,
harnessed her body to the edge of her grave,

and denied her, forever, the peace
of sinking into a romantic's yarn;

no beer drenched ballad
nor a schooner of tears, for her.

no brave heart raging
against a determined storm

no souls lost, submerging,
into davey's darkened arms.

instead, she was dropped, plainly,
into a tub of cold abandonment

where she would lie, to slowly perish,
beneath a thin sheet of raindrops,

a few lonely steps from the shore
where her fallen masts were grown,

for a sideshow crowd to come,
floating above her laid bare bones,

awed by her death shroud's clarity,
thrilled by her failure to float,

with never a song on their lips
or an echo of her ill-fated name.

the ears of small birds

my hummingbird feeder has been
hanging above the gate for months,
its red and yellow plastic is fading.
12.99 from a discount store.
the sugary mixture is slowly evaporating.
the tiny beak holes are just emptiness.

every morning, while
smoking and drinking coffee,
i watch it sway in the breeze;

>   my sentinel
>   my offering
>   my prayer

it hangs, every day, in the air
unanswered and un-noticed
by everyone but me.

praying is a song
sung in silence

which small birds can't hear.

salt

removal of form

Haiku

A truck roaring by,
A seagull squawking above,
Our day has begun.

pre-amble in the post-amble form.
for whoever cares, this piece is the
    whereever
    whatever
first piece of poetry i ever wrote. i was eleven years old
at the time
the title 'haiku' came manyyears later when a friend
who was shown it by someoneother than me pointed out the fact it is is
it? haiku
i had no idea what haiku was. i had
readsome coolshit and mimicked (mostly do mockingbird mirror)
                        (sad, pathetic, self indulgent)
                        (introspectiveretrospective)
this piece is my 'mother'
i probably hold it *too* dear, aS   IT, my mother (DONT READ INTO)
        to dear,   H
        two, *dear*
abandoned me at a veiiiiiiiiiiiiiiiiiiiiiiiiiry young age
                        foolish
                        mis-informed
i've never sounds like a long time but a mere 30 years of
writing and not writing
righting and not righting
written another haiku (it seems,
as soon as someone labelleds it **i di o d n't** want to do it
anymore)
(the poem)
this is all just fun and games till someone loses an
I*
hopefully, by the time you have read this you would have forgotten the
haiku
i'm trying......SUCKS

the cliché is the crutch of a crippled mind. Groucho Marx

37

guns akimbo

i'M AWAKE
i'M AWAKE!
      dear god
      when   -did that
you came
i will come
i will   bust
your crystal ball
s oneX1
i will wind my mind my
        WATCH
its time has cum

light is misd
directed
you blind the sun

suckle   -un holy teats
are these
new words
the new heards
the new
           birds
           flying single winged
           in circles of
           what the fuck
with ! or ? or even
.

        pick a period
        piece of language
        wrangler dangler strangler

digg!?.
ing   emo!?.
shun
Ing   clare!?.
        itty ditty shitty kitty
        ryme and tyme
        spell it out how!?.
        ever!?.
        you!?.

want-

alabaster

so there's no misunderstanding,
the world being what it is;
war breaking out, arctic seas breaking out,
love breaking out, my face breaking out,
just so we know we're on the same page,
            when
you say alabaster
            do
you mean the old sort;
the softer like skin, scratches easy, breaks easy,
sentimental pieces of poorly glued, barely holding
            or do
you mean the harder, newer form;
more resilient, can still be cut,
marked with a knife, pushed hard enough,
forced enough along its smooth surface
?
            when
you say blood
            do
you mean the river; sunset red river,
warmed by the heart of passion, pain, poetic,
            or do
you mean tissue sticky, coursing,
ever seeking the exit you created
while trying to scratch the surface
of hard alabaster
?
            when
you say fuck it
            do
you mean quietly entering dark rooms;
arms wrapped around, invisible straight jacket on,
            or do
you mean sledge hammer spinning; clenched
teeth grinding the air with resolve, landing,
grounded with a sharper focus
than a blood stained knife
?
are we on the same page
?
.

39

on the 2

left footers
in a tango of traffic

and she, with a bag of happy,
on spokes of sunshine

saw a green and took it.

she had every right,
in that way.

a gently touching happenstance.
a twisted frame.

grapes and milk: scattered, splattered.

asphalt digs into her naked knees
and infects her bloody palms.

her faith in sharing an open road
far from paralyzed,

but she limps,
and it hurts like hell.

feel the rhythm
        watch the traffic
            and step,

                 on the 2.

luvsung

it was over
the moment
       i
put
       I
on the page.

ridiculous ,
grandiose hunter
in a jungle with
a
cap gun.

the prey
flutters off the leaf
and twists manoeuvres
about eyes too slow to follow.

scientist of the soul,
attempting to pluck
a single tick of the clock
from the air with
tweezers.

arrogant,
to try and write
the definition of a word
one can't even spell.

       i
wanted to do this for
U.

(D.I.D.) *done*

fitting rain, moments split refusing, denying, separations opening as far, as daunting, as epic as the sofa to the door, everyone trying to understand the distance growing, from their eyes to the floor, slanting down, set upon to answer, hearing the accusations, like a menu, having to choose on drinks and then desert

> (it)
>   *hurt*

he once required me to hold him, without asking, through the tears, the sentences he couldn't complete, the sentence he had no choice, the way he used the cold wind, the edgy lake's plea, manipulating them like music, like faith, i did it, beyond his conviction, despite his crime, for a shorter time than it takes to recall, held him and he said thank you, he can face the separation, thank you, he will get over it, her, the years, the hurt, in time, thank you

> *i am*
>   (listening)

days, between us, them, she, i, he, i, you, i, shared, parallel, perpendicular, perfect and broken, some more than others, wrecked, smashed together, entwined as tentacles, burning and affectionate, squid, a glass of wine, three candles and good bye, so sorry, so difficult, to untangle long windswept hair, swept by the damp wind's bellowing, her sorrow, she should have left but so much between them, so many connections, to undo, so difficult to brush out this night for her, but thank you, thank you

> (time)
>   *so much* (time)

rain, we are , you and i, formless, untouchable, having a right hand for his suffering and a left for her disappointment, a face for the wind, the waves to sing to us, he having moved on, her no longer a friend, no longer caring, what's the point, really, what's left, as i, as you and i, lay back, gawking at stained, broken, hardwood, hands folded, fingers entwined, our separate nights, holding out
for whose love

> (for)
>   *who*

invitation, at last

an incoherent old man
gathering coins
to purchase a ticket
on the wrong ferry.

i close my eyes,
rushing toward an idea of touch.

i hear cracking ice
and pray for silence.

i hear my voice.
i am speaking
to myself;
to no one.

driving in the blinding snow of never knowing

47 kilometers with
out conversion   -long
ago re-conditioned
   -so many miles too many
miles   yet kilometres stretch
ing infinite beyond endless   -the
sign being the final symbol
   -i do not exist   in a vacuum

driving in the blinding
snow with its colorless
sense of humor   -whipping
about my mobile enclave
-lights and sounds
in my world now
so obviously minute

the road curves   -unex
pectedly left then
back right and left and
perhaps on a track i
wished   -to originally go
-trusting technology
E-SE-E-SE-S-SW-S-SE   No
matter how it tries to
deceive -the assault of
this storm is always head
-on

irregular weaknesses of
the insensible white
outs show the white
sky to the white field swallow
ing spruce and paupler
   -it falls and
 i catch its game in glimpses till
          back to —my
struggle —my keeping —my
head above the
flood

how not wanting it
here is longing it
there   -to walk up
  -to the waist in white
  -to stand in the white
surrounding eyes with white, ears
with white, nose skin mind with white,
heart
          with white
  -to be lost   -to be at
rest   death is usually
referred to as dark.   —is
this life ?
          ?
  -to be there in white
living death   instead
of   -this long kilometre
after kilometre of   not
knowing   -what is
coming or who is
going

i don't pheel right

pheeling as i do,
as is with most pheelings
when noticed,
they pheel strange,
pheel foreign
and now a stranger comes.

i don't pheel right.

there is too much sun
on the back of my neck;
my neck beeing exposed;
my head hanging
from my neck,
floating above my yard,
unmowed.
the sun, too long
on my exposed neck.

i don't pheel right.

a not in my muscle,
not my only muscle,
but the one beeing noticed
                most.
a muscle, tight and paining,
hidden beneath other muscles
less assertive;
a muscle pain, muscling its way
into my thoughts, my pheeling,
to the right of my exposed neck.

i don't pheel right

there is a web,
like a muscle
pulled apart and stretching out;
thin web, shimmering
like pain. i see
it, my head hanging
from my neck too long
in the sun, a strong web,

strong and having caught a bee;

a shimmering web, not
unlike all webs
i don't notice,
but i notice
this web,
notice
      the way its gotta bee

i believed the yard
was the right place.

to bee;

      for me, i be leave
      we both were wrong.

              truly,

i hang with this burn,
my neck exposed,
measuring the length
of the blade

and you, no longer
being bee or being free
in a muscle tight,
pulled and shimmering
just the same

i don't pheel right.

the theory of practicing safety pins under the influence of caramel corn (for alfred jarry)

being mean ing
is the boney fracture
faith would have you forget

tomorrow, i was reposed
and predisposed
inside the spacious confines
of this snail shell,
the beasts of reason
devouring two universes
beneath my fingernails;
how they sang me
the serendipitous truth
of the androgynous nature of rice

i rolled jupiter into a mak'em
and smoked that puppy

a blood devil i am
living dead, living ages,
living past,
sucking the hope
from a mint chocolate ice cream cone,
near luxembourg or some such
romantic long named place, when,

OH swollen teeth, OH rank beach
come love! lay not your head
on the stone of this heart;
the latch stuck, the blade
dulled cutting the furrier limbs
from words i have no use fore
head
packed in boxes to sell
saturday mornings
      (this bunch, whole box, $1.50)

while cleaning the spires of st. paul's,
flipping the cotton swab,
i looked down on you and
considered the 26 known dimensions
         (   )
and wondered
how you barely fit one

come love! do not cut my mouth
from me! do not leave me gapping!
bring forward your trembling tongue
and lick clean the scalpel
the sun used
to dissect your craving

little worm, beautiful worm.
how, now, you bring
your hardhat, lace shoes
to your hands and write me
love notes about running

i've received my pardon me,
by overnight courier,
from the office of the prime
minstrel.
bring lute! bring lyric!
come love, to my bathtub.
there, we will sail the seven seas
of meaning   nothing
of being   nothing
of being   meaning

you, me and caramel corn.

anatomy

hands:
touch blankets, dogs, skin, mud, never beating hearts hidden (**protected**),
you, water.
sunlight touches them!
they've tried, but can't grasp it,
can't pocket it,
the sunlight.
back:
long field. silk. where's mine? why does it hide?
my hands were on yours. the past.
never forward, never.
the sun touches it!
i'm not afraid.
i've seen many.
they become featureless the further away they are.
teeth:
they hurt once they've rotted.
i've neglected them before. the past!
soft enamel, the hands of words, unable to grasp
solid things, *or sunlight.*
eyes:
murky oceans of vision, longing for what's not there.
sunlight is realized only by what it bounces off.
it does not touch eyes!
eyes fear it, unlike the hand which will shield them, if they ask.
the hands always hope to stay longer.
knees:

i've bent!

soles:
hardened. workers only.
never crying *for sunlight*, like eyes.
they do as they're told-
carry the back away,
move teeth closer,
but these hands,
still wanting to hold something.
sunlight, something.

every, time

so easy to claim *i'm at war*
when the dogwood is bare
and the cracked cement
is filled with frozen decay.

i sit at this table,
profound at this table,
like this: *like a losing force.*

here is my decree, my proclamation,
my pressing conference:

i'm at war

in november,
on a moonless night
                    and i am losing.

i'm at war with
every;

tired of how it presumes;
the obnoxious way it occupies
things to become
every thing

my body, my body!
leisurely becoming
every body

the ones who've toiled
against tyranny losing.
                    all losing.

till the simple, beautiful, free ones are
every one
every body
every thing

being at war, i will fight
with every breath i have left to me.

                    i am losing.

queen street toronto \january\

i've no idea   –can't fathom
what rumors have been told
to you to cause this reticence
– was just a moment
ago when lights danced
about us   –bubble baths for
our giddy minds –your life
opened up   -the cheek of your
love firm to my palm

you cower   now   –listen
to ill advice from a sometime
friend –a drop in with cold
council;   misinformed
judgements of what i am
what you are who we are
to one   an other -voice
carries warnings with a
thick spit speaking seeming
pure but cutting to the bone

you have tucked your fine
table wares and welcome
mats   inTO dark corners
-over turn chairs   hide
them under wraps –i pass
by stop pass again
question when consistency
will bring me from the cross
road to walk un-huddled
down the length of your
affection

winter drifts in and drifts out
i wait   come by
knocking on your door –
drop notes into empty
flowerboxes   for you to find
should you ever chance
to look –to remember –to break
from the burden
of your OnAgainOffAgain house
lights.

looking down on a drowning

i'm speaking to the bent fellow
they're pulling from the lake
this morning; this early, winter morning.

futile sturgeon, grave and sodden,
listen to me.

here, in my 12th floor flat,
standing, dry and nearly naked,
behind this clear, glass wall
shielding me from the bite of the wind,

i have the perfect vantage
to be your slowly dispersing mist,
if you will have me.

and, being your ghost,
i can assure you,
we've succeeded into anonymity,
if that's what we were hoping.

now, we are known only as son,
or brother, or sorrow.

our ears are unfettered
to the trembling voices
of those who wonder
where we've gone.

we are free of the screaming
mother's song when told
we no longer drift aimless.

you are quiet, there,
in the hands of strangers

and i am quiet, here,
in the hands of no one.

and in this quiet, i'm telling you,
i will be your ghost
on this cold sunday morning.

museum of civilization, ottawa

cardinal designed his museum
without corners

all walls round and smooth
to prevent shadows

no places for
evil spirits to hide

all he's managed
is to confuse them
and piss them off

they crawl into
bill folds, purses
and souvenir bags

they follow us back to our
hotel room, causing arguments
over where to go for dinner

emperor

looking down over
concrete steps
littered with
dry leaves and twigs
spinning in a turning wind

there are ghosts
of ice creams,
of smoked cigarettes,
of neighborhood people
passing by on a saturday

i'm dressed in windows

buried beneath the burden
of windows

a full 60 watts
sustains me,
a mass market sun

i am attacked by windows

endless minutes holding me
keeping me preserved

(lang-gwij)?

what is
language
?

your illness.
your delicate torment
leaning against my open palm.
my quivering frustration
leaping between definitions.

where is
That *word* buried
for open fields;
their pale colours;
their wild and pale blooms
?

how do
They *say*
the rough ocean edge;
it's cool spray of breaking waves;
the smell of salty, drying kelp
beneath empty urchin shells
?

how can
They *say*
the hesitant, midsummer evening
dragging its drunken feet
over the threshold
of our inevitable horizon
?

what *is*
language
?

That infinite space
which crawls
between my palm
and the timid skin of your suffering
?

That wretched space
preventing my understanding
of your fading explanation
?

what is
language
but useless.

what is
language
other than
clandestine isolation
?

/dan/ger! messXen/ /ger

i was sent to you
by others:
the warbler, the wood bison,
blue whale and polar bear
and others   many others

they pinned me against
my uncompromising intellect

they threatened my life
with their own

they said

> gather leaves   =*fallen*
> gather stones   =*uncovered - grave discovery*
> gather sun   =*split - in different places*
> gather rain   =*the roadside drifting off*

they said

> *go to them*
> *tell them*
> *take this and tell them*

i've come to you
gathered as i could

i'm held
          under duress
          under stress
i must

tell you

courage my love

española

i saw her.

suddenly, i could speak spanish.
not the words, but their intent.
everything green or fire.
the hills rolling. the blue sea rolling.
the coastline with fully rigged ships.
my god! the billowing!

the short walk to the brown butcher
being all of our history of life and death.

the old woman arranging dandelions
and calling them love, hope and forever.

and it was simple.
everything
becoming simple.
the simple becoming
the most beautiful thing i ever saw.

if only i could sing,
i would be its bird.

courage, my love

The sun was going down, but you couldn't tell. It was one of those days, where the monotone light of the sky denied you any sense of time and it was dark at noon. I reached for a smoke and instead grabbed my dark round sunglasses. The ones I bought at "Courage, My Love."

Courage, that's all we need. Fuck.

I put the glasses on and reached once again for a smoke. The glasses were super polarized, so there was a bit of groping before my hand found the crushed pack I was sitting on. I popped one, which wasn't broken, into my dry mouth and struck a match.

As I lit this torch, I realised I could stare straight into the flame while it was very close to my face, so I did. I pretended it was one of those cheap movie effects, leading one scene on screen into some expository flashback.

Then, I saw, as if watching a dream, someone's face. Your face. You were sitting in that café. The one with the five dollar coffee and noveau art photographs on the wall. You were lighting one of your menthol one hundreds and, for a minute, you were Ingrid Bergman. You lit the cigarette and had trouble shaking out the match, so I blew on it.

You laughed and blew back at me. I didn't tell you, but you got drops of saliva on my glasses. I understood. I laughed.

We had just come from a movie; one about Jesus. I couldn't decide if the director was saying Jesus' death was unimportant or his film was. You looked at me, blew again and said being concerned was unimportant, so I wasn't.

Then, as though spinning through time, my match burned down and touched my present flesh. I took my glasses off and tucked them carefully into their case. I laid it on the floor next to the ashtray. I didn't like the store's monogram, "Courage, My Love," imprinted on the leather, so I turned the case over.

I took another cigarette and went looking for a lighter, so I wouldn't burn myself, again.

conjurer

do you remember,
oh,
do you remember
        what love was like

when as an
        ass backward ass
        of a conjurer

it made the world
disappear
and
its assistant more
visible
        than ever?

accidental genius

i've laid to rest
the heavy feathers
of failed flight.

away from the wind,
i tinker with the gears
of silence and jam the process
between verse and versus.

I'm looking for a clever way
to say love.
then, as an accidental genius,
i dissolve.

time ceases.
you purchase the wind.
i forget feathers.
i forget flying.

love is love. there's no other way
to say it, in prayer or out loud.

it is a heavy feather.

simple citrus

change is a tall house
shabbily built but sturdier than most
it builds itself on everything

> and this structure
> is too lofty for a poor man
> such as i

i'll not enter it

i'll go instead to the market,
placing aside such luxuries
as the ocean, the stars and the sky.

there, i'll purchase oranges,
perhaps a dozen or more,
because that's what markets are for.

they're not for understanding love
or one's self or other such noble fascinations.
i might pick up a useless bobble or two,

flippant in their color and form,
fabricated by the hands of someone
who needed a few dollars to eat.

i'll give them to you, when i return.
then, you'll read me some Susan Musgrave
and we'll cry, faced with the frightening light
of how much we understand, how much we feel,
this.

i'll tell you a story of how, in the morning,
a ghost whispered me her name
and i chose to forget it, not wanting to believe
she could exist outside my ability to touch her.

we'll peel my oranges,
my four dollar fifty seven cent oranges
and while eating them, i'll ask why you think
i didn't tell that ghost to keep the change.

swayback... chariot

where i go, goes my memory;
the memory of me.
i struggle some days
to become us; the memory of us.

opening the door of the black truck,
stepping to the cracked pavement,
walking across the busy parking lot,
to enter the crowded café, alone,

i'm a swayback pulling a heavy chariot.
the large wooden wheels carved with week days.
the basket gilded with so many mornings;
the light of those mornings.

the reigns are the ligaments of unmade choices,
tied to a bit clenched between my teeth.
i pull the sky, the moon, the rain
along. i pull my past, not ours.

standing in front of the barrista,
a small line forming behind me
i'm asked if i'll have the usual.
i neigh, not nay. i go on pulling,

trying to remember what you wanted
as you sit in the black truck. so difficult
the way you always change. so difficult
to form a memory of us one can count on.

toil

i'm tethered to a dull plow.
the straps have grown
into my shoulders and my bones.
i drag the rusted blade
through mounds of root
and over stones.

with every condemned step
i move so little earth,
and curse the empty cellar.

i count the broken jars,
reading their yellowing labels:
       'supposed to be.'
       'could have been.'
       'don't blame yourself.'

with every inch of soil i split,
i pray the day will dim.

yet, in that humid night,
the body still feels the field
crawling beneath the bed.

teasing weeds whisper
       'death does not sleep.'

nor shall i.

my mind consoles my flesh
with lies;
a redundant bedside fable

of an evening bar in buenos aires;
of a tango to tempt toes;
and the sweetened wine
of easy grapes;

of a corner table,
near an open window;

of an ocean breeze
easing papers to the floor;

of a lady, in a pale red, satin dress;
the reflection of a harvest moon;
of a happy before the home;

of a smile caressing
the edge of her glass,

of discovering a name
for every turn
of her cool and liquid skin.

of this half written letter
i was sending to my absent lover:

> "beyond these paved roads,
> the world is every shade of green.
> the night is warm
> and should be full of us;
> so full of us...."

and then the mud knocks at the door.
my spine is splintered into mulch.
the sun is not a welcome friend.
letters remain unwritten.

private beach

my island heart
breaks the surface;
floats to the top
of a sunset sea-
uninhabited, undiscovered.

no last minute packages,
nor resorts with their all
inclusive sunburn water
sports flights back and
forth daily with customs issues.

in winter, i rest on these
beaches. i listen to the smacking
kisses of these waves;

respite from the chill on my
skin.

bridle path

she couldn't keep thought
from touching the body,
preventing the inevitable kiss
between madness and the rising sun;
days mislaid in this loving regret.

the madness of regret.
as if a falling bowl would sound like bells.
as if a slamming door would sing instead of scream.
as if shadows could read their stories aloud,
coaxing a dream from beneath the bed.

the madness of sunrise.
that spinning vision of a shrinking world
rolling toward longer nights.
the growing tide of husbands and children and hope.
the long, slow journey to nothing
draped in many layers of everything.

the yolk refusing to release the plate
no matter how determined these nails dig,

the madness of everything.
family pictures on every wall.
how they hold each other,
these walls and these images.
how they touch.
      how they dance.
how they become one another,
over time.
how the colors fade
after this love making.

how the pressed sheets
wrap a stale mattress
with a promising scent
of rose and rest.
through every season.
through thick and thin.

reach

i have not left the world
i wander for a time
the winding corridors
of want   searching
for comfort against
the anguish of ambiguity

my eyes open eyes open   see
only real things,
knot their negative shapes

only taste bland
                spices not the stinging bee

i trip endlessly   with
out inspiration
i write with
out having
anything
too say, too speak,
the words are gone to their gods
to complain   they have been
served an injustice by my unsound
ideas,

i want a tongue to scream

i want a hand to touch you

rage burns the tender tips
of verbal weeds, extending to
an unforgiving sun,

it wants its
dew as
well.

the licence to be poetic is
about to be suspended, like like like
polleninamber

the ember cracking with
the mind's inability
to mould a clearer image.

i have crawled through
the books, the letters
the masters, the teachers, the sages

the dead

they speak clear, they speak
ancient spells, but I cannot get my
crooked grey matter to matter
anymore.

words have returned
to gods, to complain;
to appeal for a new charge on
some other page, their use
wasted on silly concoctions
bottled by a carpet bagger;
peddled town to town

whose dignity is smeared

the mud of rain soaked
paths cutting forests cover
their loveliness against
desires
to capture them, they wait for
an artist, a sensitive to
coyly whisper adulations and
seductions to them, in the
dull quiet of the morning
they bath in the thin waters
of nights wet lips

i waste   time, i waste   blood, i waste

the spit which flies as i bellow
spells into the empty spaces
between reach and beauty

my voice falls short and shorter
as the distance grows the closer i be

come

i chase down the heavy beast
of living

with both hands
gripping tight its tail
it drags me deeper into
a spiral wood
i don't understand

the sun has left
now
it has had enough of
my obtusely angled ideas

my cries for its love;
morose mumblings

i see yUo. i really do

the hounds of loss
gather at my door.

through its rotting wood
they've stumbled onto the scent
of the empty chair
shrinking against the wall.

i have everything
piled in the hall,
to keep them out.

the ocean rose, leaving behind its salt
and rode an empty sky to fall on me.

every drop, Every Drop,
one word of our language;
one letter of your name.

it's always night
when a dear friend suffers
in body.

it's always three a.m.
when i gather the silence
which filled yesterday.

it's always early morning
when i listen for any swish,
any tapping, any whisper
or whoosh of you passing.

these hounds howl and claw.

i'll *not* let them in!

this is prayer

i cry openly
listening to *Redemption Song*
with my ipod headset,

as i stoop
to gather the shit
my dog has left
on the walk outside of
your house.

this is not poetry.
this is prayer.

pussy willow

but what i should
have said was cat tails
windswept; bending,
long and drying, dying.
        oh, how i love
        your dark
        side. how you
        don't say what
        you say. how you
run an icy finger,
slowly, down my
spine, spine, spine:
from cerebellum to
the grave.
        oh, how i love your
        ghostly touch. touching
        as if attacking. yes,
        i pinched that, blatantly.
a singer must die. judge
me. judge. judge.
        oh, how i love the
        longing. the death
        without the silence.
        the sentence, gladly
        taken. a touch
        of hemlock in the
        ear, ear, ear.
i did say cat tails,
forgetting in the
speaking
        oh nine
but that's next -
year after year after
stone upon stone
upon stone upon stone.
        oh, how i love
        the throwing up
        and up they rise.
        throw them and i will
        gladly be buried
below.

the widows of lisbon (memory)

it's not time to follow her.

others have,
from sunlight to shadow;
down alleys with
shuffling footsteps.

she wears her black kerchief
and tattered sweater.
she carries bags of hard bread.
she mumbles prayers.
she misses him.

the steady men gripping cervasia
on a saturday afternoon know her.

they know her well.
they knew her man.
they watch her pass.

she's stolen the eyes,
the hands and the voice
of many poets watching
as she speaks to the soil;
as she kisses the cold, grey stone.

she is not death.
she's an old woman in a kerchief,
carrying bags.

she is not death.
she is the memory of it.
the one who calls her lover,
does so in silence.

she is the soil she speaks to.
the night hugs her skin.
she caresses, gently, that night.

it's not yet time to follow her,
but i see, clearly, where she goes.

veil

with steam pouring from an iron,
she hovers over a thin landscape
of embroidered hope
and flattens a bridal shroud,
working ancient threads
with a surgical skill.

a curtain of innocence
lost in a mother's history.

not her mother, but mine.

how the years in a cedar box
have sewn themselves
into a sentimental cocoon;
now opened, never again knowing
the heartbeat of a thankful moth,
wrapped up in its folds.

despite the holes marauding teeth
have made through out,
the silk border and wispy patterns,
have not lost any glow, nor moved
even a little from its absolute white.

> *i see, in the unfocused air between us,*
> *the pudgy fingers of my young sister,*
> *flapping the veil over our mother's queen size bed,*
> *then draping that cloth over her small girl head.*
>
> *she seemed to vanish, down to her feet.*
> *'ghost', i called her 'you look like a ghost.'*
>
> *then my mother reclaimed her day*
> *from about my sister's careless youth,*
> *and with surgical skill, turned that circle*
> *back into a square.*

my determined wife, now, gathers the largest part
of this lovely rag toward the center
of a large, thin, velvet board, which is resting
in a larger frame.

i see how she hides every chewed emptiness;
how she weaves clouds; how she arranges
the patterned edges like a painted wind;
coaxing it's unwillingness with pearl tip pins,
until it settles into a flattering shape.

'oh, look at that' she says,
and lifts her hours of work
before me.
 she asks "what do you think?"

and there it is, once again,
a circle in a square.
no holes, no tears.
every wound neatly tucked
away.

i see an afternoon moon.

i see how she's raised the dead.

the waiting silence broken (a glosa)

my hands reach back to meet this despair,
and the frozen rain shreds the flesh from bone as I watch,
transfixed by the undoing of corporeal illusion.
To tendon, to bone, to dust and release.

The Despair   *Dale Winslow*

the waiting silence broken

the shore is at rest.
the soil and sea don't quarrel any longer.
nothing; nothing moves. the starfish
lies tranquil in a clear shallow pool.
the herring gull pauses on a mossy rock.
the mist ceased struggling with the air.
the sun is providing only light.
it holds back its heat. the day will never end.
everything lingers, silent, without you there.
my hands reach back to meet this despair.

in the long emptiness of holding on,
at the edge where ebbing and flowing
won't look to one another,
won't utter a sound for fear
of tipping the spinning plate of anticipation,
i, in Heraclitus's water, resolve to bellow and clutch
the lever of hope and pull. everything jumps,
frightened awake, toward the night.
the sun fades. the sky turns quickly to rust
and the frozen rain shreds the flesh to bone as I watch

now, i'm an intolerable child;
having been revealed impetuous and impatient,
i've become a standing oblivion,
as i could not keep my fingers
from the delicate crystal of your rebirth.
these tender moments tremble at my intrusion.
the room you left clear and polished
breaks as glass, burns as timber
and i, (witness, victim and criminal) stand in confusion
transfixed by the undoing of corporeal illusion

the ink of my voice runs dark and thick.
the pigment of my vision fades.
the trust you placed in me is painful to touch.
i lower my head as the willow bends its branch;
settled, abandoned in the waiting.
the echo of beauty my only relief.
i look to these joints and sinew and blood;
to the skin hanging loosely to flesh;
as time comes to take it, piece by piece.
to tendon, to bone, to dust and release.

death

death
is a group of words,
not a single syllabic utterance:
(hard at first -
-drifting off softly at the end).

death is a phrasing
in a run on sentence
devoid of any adjective
other than endless.

death has become a cry;
a dark reflection;
no longer symbolic
of change.

thorough. sudden.
expected, but surprising
none the less.

> death
> has lost its romance,
> now encapsulated in therapy
> and in panicked relations.

death, personified, walks
a lonely path, miss-understood,
and modernized by science.

its relegated to the same
crumbling building
as gods - as god - as myth...

there were moments
when death and love
equalled the song
poets would sing for you.

> it no longer
> sweeps and sways and wanders.

death will wait quietly
at the bank of the river
next to the mums
and you – us – i – we will
embrace it

one time;
never forgetting;
never letting go.

no?

her not answering the question
gave me a moment to consider
those inanimate objects
we play with from time to time :

the week-end paper, the remote control,
coffee machines, lawn mowers,
death;   occasionally,
how we pronounce love,
as if to the common man

they remind me of this room:

with two love seats, a coffee table,
old pictures of some people
alive or gone (what suits your fancy)

me in this room, you in this room
with me, from time to time,
perhaps
even you in this room alone, i don't know

not being there, at those moments
i'm in the yard
considering those animated things
which bounce about outside of us:

those cumbersome bees
on the wisteria, legs thick with pollen

dogs barking complaints of
imprisonment over fences

sunny side up chamomile flowers
and two swallow tail butterflies

see, how they are dancing or attempting
to love or trying to rip one another's wings off?
either way,
it's all quite beautiful to watch

from a distance.   no?

devout

her night is a catacomb,
piled with anxious bones,
shadows of long neglected
disappointments,
looking to buy their way
into her after life.

she smiled yesterday.

it fluttered,
       as smiles sometimes flutter,
       as certain, bright colors.
       then it left.

it's difficult to understand
why the ocean continues
to move as it does,
yet it does, with or without our awe.

such is her heart
and the cocooning caterpillar.

and testament

there is the hallelujah chorus!
i'm blind to your aching,
my eyes pierced by your stiletto finger,
but my ears still hear the clanging bells
of your ruined cathedral.

the final note of your melody
was slightly off key;
let me fix this for you.

death embraces life,
and life embraces death;
the original lovers;
the greatest understatement;
they have, forever and forever,
only had eyes for one another.

there is nothing dirty in their affection.
they are equally beautiful.
they are equally perfect.
they are equally embracing solitudes;
the penultimate paradox.
they are both my friends,
and i support them.

shadows are their playful children;
never black or white,
but an elusive grey, a fading tone.
these gentle offspring
only find substance
in an abundance of light.

why would we fear them?
why would we chastise them?
why would we pretend
they can dance in absolute darkness?
i embrace these lonely, misunderstood hearts
as god-children.

i've always limped, as have you,
and i Will not deny a certain crutch.
i Will find support where i can,
and i Will walk where i wish;
my stick being the giant red wood
of those who have loved the same;
those who also refused these words
being anathema:
poetry, poet, poem and love.
those who knew definition
was the second greatest paradox;
nothing ever definite.

and love: sweet love has revealed itself
as an ocean? as a sky? as tears?
i AM an archaeologist of romance,
and the bones are buried in you.

this is the greatest love:
i love because i can;
not for gain, or for your love returned;
not for satisfaction or for affection.
you do not need to notice my love.
you do not need to know me.

you can burn my love, you can burn
my picture, you can bury my bulb,
but i will love you, and you and you
because i can.

open the door to your empty house.
show me the outline on the wall
where your head hung in dust.
show me the kitchen sink,
half filled with murky water,
and the name ocean roughly scratched
on the wall behind it.

get away

it was a weekend
   get away.

the entire family
   came along.

     the mall was a lot of walking.
     the hotel was dirty.
     there was no room service.
     six people in a car built
     for four.

in three days,
   i shot 14 rolls of 36 exposures.

i saw nothing.
   i developed none.

pig and whistle

sunday evening melancholy
knows nothing of manners.
it has no respect for hunger
and has dug its crooked finger
into my tired spine.

the beans go into the pot
by the bag, and are eaten
by the spoon.

i've not moved beyond the scent
of wood burning in a stove
elevated on black victorian legs,
above a faded linoleum floor.

it's an easy thing
losing your way about the kitchen,
breaking one of the good bowls,
in tears, over an orphaned memory.

easier than molasses,
warmed on toasted, fresh bread
  (*no cure for fever but a good sign
  of how far you've come through
  by how sweet it tastes.*)

it's as easy as walking across
the dim parlor carried by
the seductive scent of mahogany,
warm electricity and lemony pledge.

easy as turning the dial,
three clicks to the left,
on the black and white zenith.

it's as easy as leaning across the table
pushing the laptop out of the way,
and responding to the question
"what's a pig and whistle?" with

"that's for me to know
and you to find out."

89

departures

i walked away from
my family,
in formative years;
walked onto a train;
walked away from any
hope of return.

i walked away from
your holy spirit;
from safe harbour
against wind and rain;
walked away from any
hope of salvation.

i walked away
from random passions
walked away from variety,
to stand still as a stone
tangled in deeper reaching roots.

do i tie my shoes with this;
walking away from
the comfort of knowing
an arm may hold me
at my death?

i think this, as i tie
my shoes, in early
morning, to go walking
in the cold.

to walk in the cold, until
it hurts.

i've grown fond of walking.

i've grown fond of away.

i've grown fond of the cold

cycling

1.
       there are times
we cradle memories in our arms
like dead children.

we call them angels.

we ask ' is that me?'

we become a colourless picture
we stumbled across in an old magazine.

we place the book on the table
and wish we had never seen it.

my life, my language,
is no longer the morning.
it's a shirt too small and no clean socks.
it's choking on old coffee,
sucked while trying to breathe.
it's the dizziness after the first cigarette.

2.

i want to ride my bike.

i want to dig it out from behind the shed,
oil the rusty gears
and tighten the handle bars,
not caring about the holes
mice have chewed into the seat.

i want to be a too tall boy

ripping down a hill,
standing up into a wind i create
on a windless day.

i want to live that life
for an unsaved child;
for what i carry
in my tired arms.

will you forget? (a glosa)

Come not, when i am dead
To drop thy foolish tears upon my grave
To trample round my fallen head
And vex the unhappy dust thou wouldst not save.

COME NOT, WHEN I AM DEAD...   Alfred, Lord Tennyson

will you forget?

every mother, with every tear unshed
on empty, winter evenings,
wander through their forsaken kitchens,
passed their worn and empty chairs
while rubbing dry and crooked fingers
(which felt the fevers and made the bed)
to lock the locks against the midnight
and every day add to their list
the thousand ways it can be said,
'Come not, when I am dead'

oh lord of mercy, or so she taught,
is there redemption for our sin
of favouring blindness when asked to see?
should we seek pardon from an echo
or compassion from a ruthless memory?
are we, forever, to be sorrow's slave?
 nightly, the choir sings in our dreams,
'how you learn, when you have no choice,
to walk, now, slowly (so well behaved),
To drop thy foolish tears upon my grave.'

name, after name, after name, is lost
to the long, hollow pain of history.
yet the word by which we called you
in times of want, and especially need,
could never be etched in eroding stone,
nor on any plaque, ever be read.
so, here, in the chapel of your demise
your choir sings, with every right,
'mourn your loss of needle and thread,
To trample round my fallen head'

sing, multitude of voices from gathering years!
we lay ourselves down in a blanket of tears
and press our ears to that heavy box,
listening, as you're lowered into that muddy pit,
"will you forget a love, such as I could feel,
bequeathed to me, which I, then, freely gave?
will you forget my hope and then my pride in you?
will you forget my arms and my comforting breast?
will you forget our sea, our shore, and our wave
And vex the unhappy dust thou wouldst not save?"

ungloved

When we were on the bus, last night, coming back from the fair, I was looking toward the window, but not at the passing people outside. I've seen enough of those monoliths. No, I was looking at your reflection, twisted toward my reflection. Tonight was different.

There were no breathless ranting about philosophies. There were no names of dictators, kings or rock stars spoken. We just looked in the same direction; toward the night.

I felt your gloved hand come to a rest on my knee. I look down then, quickly, up to your eyes to see, perhaps, some faint trace of motive or decision, before they rush back into the recess of your mind. But, I only saw. I only saw....

I put my hand on your hand and the oily feel of your leather glove shocked my good intentions. So, I took the glove from your fingers and put it in my pocket. Once again, I put my hand on your hand which resumed its position on my leg.

I played with the thin ring on your little finger, all the time staring at your hands sudden nakedness and asked you, my voice creaking in its effort to be quiet ,

" What do you think of...of...do you think that..."

You flipped your hand over and closed your palm on my palm, raised it slowly up to your face and regarded it, like it was some birth mark or mole you never noticed you had in all your years of life. You look at me, quickly, to see some part of the shadow of rational thought and through the reflection of your eyes in the window, I saw that you saw.

Last night on the streetcar, I opened my eyes and saw many things I've never seen before and now, today, I sit on the edge of the lake and stare at the orange hue of a slow sunset. I reach, because of the bitter, coastal breeze, to put my hands into the pockets of my long coat.

My good intentions are shocked by the feel of your oily, leather glove, buried deep and close to my loose change.

fold and slip

After reading Charles Simic's "my noiseless entourage"

56 of 65

is the page where i stopped reading
Simic's book. i couldn't advance
further, blinded as if driving
west into the naked sun.
(I can't simply say *brilliant*)

he's old. i'm merely almost.
he owns thousands of words
and the title to the hectares
of ideas they roam. i rent cement
near a slaughter house of acronyms.

my efforts are holes in water
and his a tub: filled to the brim,
hot and tightly plugged. without
meaning to, his pages judged me.
perhaps I asked to be sentenced,

standing, dumbfounded and awkward,
unable to finish crossing the road,
as his solid vehicle ran me over
and left me flat, on a broken line,
bloating.

carmen of bucharest

on the evening of my best intentions,
i am more I than i had hoped to be.
faced with a corporation of witches
at the base of the stairs,
i conclude ascendance is not vital
compared to all the pleasure lost
determining how many happy days
may be left to me.

before this blue-grey winter is done,
i'll find a tiny table
with two mismatched chairs,
a lidless teapot
with two tea cups,
(the nearest one chipped on the rim).
i'll boil water on a borrowed flame.
i'll steep a dark and heavy brew
to run between what remains of teeth
floating loose in resigning gums.

i'll draw a stranger from a tumbling mass
and fashion him into a dear companion.
he'll be wearing those trousers which fit
and shoes beneath, which match his shirt.
of course, he's *been* to bucharest,
where all the women are beautiful;
where all the beautiful women pass by,
and in passing by, their passing by
makes love to us forever.

my companion enquired, once,
of one specifically beautiful woman,
a specific question
about cigarettes or museums or coffee.

her response was a song her hair danced to.
it danced on the summer breeze,
when the summer had a breeze.

it drifted close enough to touch his face.
it wound tight about his life.
it cocooned him in a silky web
and left him stranded, hanging,
suspended in eternity.

now, he's comfortably reclined
in our makeshift cafe,
on the stable legged chair
and i on the wobbly one.
he tells me these facts, facts
to fill my mind.

i pour him his black tea.
we'll consider, till the longest hour,
the word *inevitable*;
its necessity.

i've fancied his trousers
in better days,
but there's little to be done
about it now.

the depth of her lake

they laid a veil on the face of Ophelia
     when she was heaved from the murky pond
when her heart was pulled from the mud
     when her broken mind, the mind they broke, was gathered,
the pieces scattered about the bed of the fallen rose.
     they laid to rest the aching breast
of the child she wanted to be,
     the woman which crawled from time
the love she believed she knew;
     they carried her to the highest hill,
cleared of all its trees; bereft of the sun
     and left her there for the sparrow to see
they called the sparrow, the sparrow, the sparrow
     and the tears and moans became the song,
the song, the song of the sparrow they called.
     it settled down to the heart of her matter
carried the shards of her dream to the nest
     laid to rest the bits of her voice
which could not be heard
     beneath the wave,
beneath the skin of the lake.
     they stood and stared, they did not dare
to walk too near to the shroud
     which billowed as sails as clouds as smoke
as rain blown harsh against the glass;
     which billowed toward a forsaken god
a god, a god whose eyes they gouged
     long before they sent her away
to drown in the hate of a silent lake,
     the lake the lake which did not pay
but took the words she hoped to pray,
     which did not care and would not hear
the pleas beneath the wandering night,
     the night, the night, the night
the night.

samson

1.

delilah
freed her honeysuckle scented skin
and melted it inside the flame
of samson's heated temperament .

she did as she desired.

she leaned against his mountain,
daring it to move;

'bury me,' she softly said,
'take me to your lonely pit.'

that was then,

> but cowards said,

> *he'll kill us all.*

> *he'll shake his fist
> into this cloud,
> a flood he'll open
> above our heads.*

> *your body is the key.*

> *turn it in his locks,
> and steal a measure
> of his collapse.*

> *consider who we are.*

> snails council well,
> while deep inside the shell.

she did as she was asked.

2.

stumbling to his grip,
she wondered as she fell,

'what story have we begun?
what sentence do i end?

i haven't the strength,
not like they think.

what makes you what you are?
should you have let me in?'

he had a heart, a tear, a hand,
and she was safe with them.

3.

the wine quivered,
as it approached her lips.
the heavy head of hopelessness
resting on her breast.
she weaved his vines
through her fingertips.

'what more could they want?
he's no beast, here, in our bed.
the only threat is in our hips.

how has it come to this?'

he had a touch, a song , a kiss,
and she drifted off with this.

4.

'love,' she said. love she meant.

'i'm flipping coins inside the fist
of a dark and silent lie;
a cheap exchange from a foreign land,
without a merchant, close at hand,
having time for us to buy.'
'love,' she said.

love she meant.

'you are my house;
my balcony;
the breathing landscape
of my dreams,

yet it means nothing,
as we are shackled
to the cart
of a living history.'

'love,' she said.
love she meant.

'who are you? who am i?
on the sword of whose conviction
must we die?

am i the sulphur on the match,
or the stone that's striking it?'

he had a sky, a smile, a breeze,
and she was willing to live with these,

     but they returned,

     he'll kill us all
     remember this
     as you whisper
     in your sin

     you will do as you were asked
     for the silver and the gold
     you will do as you were told
     or this night may be our last.
     this night will be your last.

     snails council best
     when others do the rest

5.

delilah,
being the wrong inside his right,
begged him to reveal,
'what am i to do?'

then samson said,
'you will become the unwed bride,
the alter waiting near your side,
and i the lamb upon its slab;
a remnant of the life i had.

i will become the bleeding knee
and you the sweet of a stinging bee.
you will take my strength and my sight.
you will take my day, and give me night.

we will do this, and they will leave
the voice of love, adrift at sea.
you will be the water, i will be the sand,
if you will hold me in your hands

when the knife and chains arrive;
when i am split, dead and alive,
then, you will become the moon at night
ever fading, from left to right.'

'love,' she said.
love she cried.

'i will touch no hair on your head,
nor drive a nail into your eyes,
but rest your ear, near my lips,
and fill it with a long good bye.

come others.
come lurking shadows.
come lesser men.
come scissors.
come shame.
come morning.
come pain.

there is nothing left to say'

Tennyson's tomb

such a lovely volume of water.
embossed crimson leather,
small enough for one hand.
the thin, yellowing pages with
the small font, singing like a boys' choir.
his lily lay inside, tightly pressed,
sleeping in that lake of time,

until a hand, swinging a rattle of feathers,
tried to clear the settling dust
from off his crowded perch,
and he fell: he fell,
like a bag of stones,
onto the hardwood floor and shattered.
his spine being dry and bent,
he simply couldn't hold it together
any longer.

would the spirit of mary black
leap off her hand written order form,
tucked in the front cover, and judge me?
how long had she pinched, in 1907,
to have this jewel of love sail
across an impossible ocean,
to give her lamp light reason to burn?
would she curse my recklessness?

i was at a loss. how do i, now,
keep Tennyson from drifting
about the house; from tucking under
baseboards and settling behind cushions;
wrinkling his skin beneath sheets.
the verse was loose and i was at risk
of not being able to bind it again.
what was i to do?

i called out for help! i declared a state!
i asked for some unused, small chest
to gently place these broken phrases in.
i was handed the only thing there was
and i paused.

'oh my words, who will judge me now?'

i laid poor, torn Tennyson
in an empty hallmark gift box
with a tiny pink bow,
and buried him, carefully,
at the back of the book self.

fold lily. fold and slip.

gravediggers

I

bring out the dead.
moments, once
coursing with flow
now
still.

i lay them, forever,
apart
in neat rows
      in a snow pale
      flat field.

some, neglected in
distant corners.
others, tended to.

      all eventually forgotten,
      if not for these

time faded, rain damaged
stone sentinels.

i clear these bodies.
i keep them from lying
about,
reducing the possibility
of infection.

<u>II</u>

in spring
>   neck deep in
>   a mud pit, rain a
>   drain on resolve
>   they dig.

in summer
>   bared flesh, sweat,
>   hammering hard,
>   dry earth, slowed by
>   cantankerous roots
>   they dig.

in autumn
>   with a practiced
>   rhythm, fading
>   days and dull images
>   give way to mind
>   numbing effort.
>   it begins to make
>   sense with the
>   dying light
>   harmonized with
>   the dying with in
>   they dig

in winter
>   waiting. ice is an
>   aggressive foe.
>   the cold is a tyrant,
>   a bully, making
>   stronger muscles
>   atrophy in the
>   waiting for
>   an existential
>   thaw
>   they stop
>   in winter.

they wait as
more arrive, and
the silence grows.

III

as wind blows,
    the earth opens
    slow.

we sing, quietly.
    no lament.
    a work song.
    a digging song.

the leaves dance.
    the earth opens
    slow.

we prepare this ballroom,
this white sheet, a table
dressing, on which to
set a banquet for
Hero

for her moments
    now coming home

which moved us
    now coming to stay

which held us
    now coming to rest

for Hero,
coming home
    from her heartbroken shore.

IV

they will be kept

                 here   and here   and here

on this bed.
        this white shroud,
        spread, cleaned and pressed.
        perfumed.

they will be laid

                 here   and here   and here

        in the open air,
placed close and dressed,
        revered.

they can be viewed

                 here   and here   and here

        in clear sight.
never missed.
        sustaining.

V

he digs
with

          honor,
          humility,
          respect,
          love,
          peace,
          determination.

he digs
knowing

          he won't be the last
     believing
          when he needs his rest
          someone will be there
          to tuck him in
    with
          honor, humility,
          respect, love, peace,
          a determination
          to keep his yard
          as flat, white, and clean

          as he first found it.

          he will join, as brother,
          those memories he has
          laid to rest.

he will
know,

          the backbreaking,
          callous ripping,
     work
          he and his loyal
          companion, the earth
          endeavoured to do
          has led to
          Victory.

so he digs
these graves.

the trenches

sunrise has rusted,
ceasing morning in awkward angles.
i bend against an unwilling spine,
despite the protest marching
up and down the length of my years.

in this dragging, staggering hour,
the black wind, which has stalked me,
lurks beyond the leaf and vine.
i smell the earth's sweet blood
drying on its nocturnal chin.

i move to the ravaged garden's edge,
with a vast army of effort at my back.
i raise my fist and my voice
"onward, always onward!
we'll carry the lame and their limbs!"

a few stay back and bury the dead.

dust to dust

in our silent agony,
the night passes
without mercy.
our dusty bodies unfold
away from one other.
our twisted limbs
are desperate roots,
clawing at a stony ground.

the glass-less window
offers no escape for flesh
without the will
to rise and run.
there's no pardon
in the hands of a wind,
which whistles and taunts
our uncovered suffering.

if i dream of swollen citrus,
its seeping liquor running
the length of its tree's bark,
its sticky pool of moisture
gathering on the soil,
collecting in a heavy shade

if i dance my tongue
over and through this juice

if i dream of this silence dying,
and the heated breeze cooling,
alongside waves somersaulting
in an open and playful way,
without shame

if i connect one finger's tip
to your otherness,
will we swell and drip,

or flake and drift away?

thin lines

digestion

your mouth
was full of last night's
conversation.

with a finger,
i traced the line
dividing your full lips.

a digestive
for the words
you still chewed on.

dog

and your breath
has the scent
of living death.

your eyes fill
with twilight

and still you know me,
leaning in your private darkness
toward my voice

i'll lie with you
and offer you my bent nails
to chew on.

you taste the salty life
buried on my skin

your slow jaw,
with your softened teeth,
tries to hold on

and finally

there is an understanding
between us
between our bodies

all lines are erased

one moment,
we can breathe:
one moment…

gooseberry cove

1.

it's always grey on the coast.

2.

there are some lines
which have no meaning.

i have one, here,
in the handbook of my soul.

i have recited it, every day,
for over twenty four years

and i know for certain
it has no reason.

3.

it is one thing to say you don't fear,
till that drifting, body-less shadow
lays its eternal darkness against
the cheek of someone else
and asks you to play the music
they will dance to.

4.

she needed to get away
and asked if i would take her.

it had been weeks,
since my old friend and i
had been together.

it would be good, to get away.

5.

a loose assembly of players:

the life:
she bellowed from her gut,
toward the unhearing ears
of the unfaithful, uncaring betrayer,
on the morning before.

a half a bottle of chivas:
hidden in a backpack,
not to drink, but to sweeten
the lips of the salty waves.

a handful of lupins:
she insisted we stop
at the side of the highway,
so she could gather them,
to lay on the grave
of her womb.

bare feet:
on the slick stone
and wet heather slope of
a path, thin and muddy,
trodden by so many
before her.

rings, bracelets and two coins:
sentimental trinkets he gave her,
to be tossed into the throat
of a rising tide.

the voice of those waters:
of the ghosts which live there
calling her, and only her,
to come and be held.
forever held.

my trembling voice:
my reaching hand
begging for hers. begging her
to come back from the edge.

my unwillingness:
to be her sweet chariot.
had i known.

the cold:
lasting kiss of the north Atlantic.

a few tears:
for nothing

6.

she etched her masterpiece
in the granite foundation
of my memory,
in one dimension:
it having only width,

and try as i do,
i cannot get around it,
nor scratch it out.

7.

it's one thing to say you don't fear
till that drifting, body-less shadow
asks you to play the music.

8.

her broken body
did not die, that day,
but everything else did.

i've tried, over time, to see myself
as the mooring post
holding her listing ship
against the tide,
but, i merely held a body back,
which was emptied.

everything was gone,
irretrievably at the bottom
of the beckoning atlantic..

highwaymen

when suffering lay down
over the sharp exhaust grate,
on the breath of hell's lungs,
in a blanket of ghostly hands,
warmer than the wind created
by the blind rushing by
(blind with a life, blind with contempt)
i was one of those who walked by.

what, under that heap of rags,
buried against the coming night,
had the courage to stretch their hand
out across the road of stampeding feet,
risking errant boots crushing bones,
to loosely grip a small box with
a few coins stressing the negative shape
where the cold had settled down?

and here we are, presuming
this is about the homeless, but,
it is not. i tell you, it is not.
i walked, swiftly,
from that thin thread hanging
from the worn sheet of history.
this is about a racoon.

about the failing heap of a racoon,
stretched across the broken white line
of the highway i'm travelling down.
one small leg, still twitching in the air,
the only thing moving, waving me down,
warning me off, fearing my blindness,
reaching for the other curb,
plucking every sense of safety
from the air entering my lungs.

highwayman, with your final fist in the air,
punching from that murky sea of shadows and fur,
as you drown in darkness, you, too, presume.
i couldn't pass five dollars, or a sandwich,
to the hardened image further up the line
and you would have me pause and notice you.
i have no stomach for your condition.
i have no ability to affect your mortality.
i've not even words for you.
i've not even eyes.

and still, we presume
this is about road kill.
it is not. i tell you, it is not.
it's about me. it's about you.
it's about desolation. it's about how,
in our electric light and glowing warmth,
we may never understand it,
nor accurately express it.
so...

here, take my hand.
together, we'll walk, swiftly,
from these thin threads and broken lines.

man

it was an odd death,
having crossed that thin line
not as the body
but, as the accident.

I, as
an older boy,

in a rage, placed my hands
on the chest of my father,
to the heart of his matter,
and pushed him away.

it was that simple.
as simple as the coffee table
behind him, when he fell back
across it; arms splayed wide.

it was that solid.
as solid as the sound
of breaking glass
beneath the weight
 of my falling giant.

my glorious sandcastle,
dissolving in a wave.

it was that sudden.
as sudden as a foot
on black ice, under snow;
as a thumb beneath
the hammer's head;
as a tongue between
clenched, broken teeth;
as a light at the end
of a switch.

suddenly,
i was blocks away,
standing in an empty lot.

a torn sweater.
a pair of house slippers.
a hard uncaring ground.
a shocking clarity.

arriving at a place
where I was to become
now and forever a man
in my own skin

my own cold and shivering skin.

the lover's eye

i spent a moment
in and about
my lover's eye.

not any eye,
but the right eye.

the eye seen most clearly
when hurt, disappointed
or simply lost,
she turns from me.

shut, now, while she sleeps
i walk the thin line.

i look for a breach
where i might crawl inside
and wave the colorless flag
of my nation's regret.

how i long to trade
across that border.

pulled by the gravity
of her minor globe.

buried in the depth
of her snowy world.

like any bulb in its garden
it blooms;
the colors smoothing the edges
of any storm's alarming dark.

like any bulb, in its socket,
it shines when switched on
and, equally, will dull and fade
when the room is emptied
and the electricity of the moment
is damned up at the switch.

nuclear

with a glowing heart, you made me
convert my popsicle stick in a puddle
to a battleship
because a reagan was to be a president
and there were *others*, called communists,
and they were going to slam
against one another
and here i was, between them
and they couldn't see me

with a glowing heart, you made me
read books with shiny titles
filled with even more *others*
with nowhere to go,
and they wanted to settle
on my shelves and in my dreams
and everything was going to burn
and i couldn't stop them

with a glowing heart, you made me
wear red, plastic flowers, to put that
bullet hole on my chest with pride
and the legion hall of twice dead men
on dorchester street was more
than a place to eat cake
on our nation's birthday

with a glowing heart, you made me
memorize maps, with mesmerizing
blues and reds and yellows,
showed me how the world was divided,
taught me to color inside the lines
and only later told me
what those colors meant

and now, shining as bright as i can
i find it hard to forgive you,
for what you made
and all the years it took to undo it
because you, or your offspring,
are still teaching
with a pile of cake in your mouth.

woman

1.

with one staggering drop
of a kiss
she drew a line in my sand.

she said,
'this is innocence'
and
'this is longing',
then dared me to cross.

2.

on a long summer's day,
she asked me to walk backwards
around her house, thirteen times,
so she could see the devil
sitting on the roof
and, i couldn' t do it.

so she led me,
hand in hand by hip,
to old Andy's rhubarb patch;
begged me to taste
how sweet jam
was once a sour weed.
she begged me to eat it all
and, i could not do it.

she knew this : i didn't

she laid back on the earth ,
between rows of rhubarb and elephant ears,
and removed her sweat shirt,
revealing to me what else she had found.

beneath the red sun and green leaves,
their colors bleeding on us,
her skin became stained glass
and i became a blind beggar;
reminded my god was watching.

she said 'lie down and touch me'
and i couldn't do it.
god knows,
i could not.

3.

on a long summer's day,
i asked her to revisit our garden
and she showed me her shoes:
how shiny they'd become;
showed me her skirt:
how it had grown legs.

she said,
'I'm dating Joseph'

and i replied,
'i'll make the devil
come sit on the roof,
if that's what you want.'

and i heard,
'that's just a fable.
you could never do it.'

she knew this.
i didn't.

i looked toward my feet
and saw the line
drawn in the sand
and,
i was divided.

communion

every step we take is to foreign territory, as was going to dinner
at my fiancé's for the first time. the straight back chairs propping me up
against the table. the walls propping the chairs against me. the pictures of
strangers propping the walls against history.

it was here, painted into the background of the first supper, i understood
my difference.

spicy chicken delicately disassembled. a fragrant yellow root glistening.
odd, long buns cut in half, longing for a buttery salve. all these things
becoming tones for a language i couldn't flatten out.

i remember her mother, repeatedly, checking my tolerance for the heavy
stock of their people with 'do you like?'
     yes, thank you. it's good

with my fiancé's hand squeezing my knee, she sang her strange song of
family;
the r's rolling and the vowels elongated at the end of each word, like a
thread being dragged through my mind, sewing up any holes my thoughts
might escape from.

without warning,

they changed their tune to a broken version of mine. it was here i
understood
belonging and i knew i didn't. each, in turn, recounted stories, sitting
around their table like a council chamber.

they told tales about childhood; about aunts and uncles; about
grandparents;
each story practiced and honed.

overlooked details were filled like an ill-fitting window stuffed with
tissue,
no matter how small the draft. mistakes were never faulted because
mistakes were never made.

stories poured out, hour after hour, as if their bodies needed to free
themselves of surplus, making space for the history being composed this
night.

it was here i understood being foreign.

their common lives were a country. their bodies were villages connected
by days stretched out into highways.

their ability to recount them was a passport, a key for a door,
clearly and confidently declaring 'i belong here'. and i knew i didn't

we entered the family room, where they settled against each other;
their papers having been checked and verified.

it was here i understood my pockets were empty and my documents
forged.

her father brought me a glass of port; asked me to a quiet place; asked me
to a separate place; asked me to sit at his bar;

began to tell me about his sons - the troubles he has with them; about his
house-
the troubles he has with it; about his daughter and how he loves her, how
he is afraid.

it was here that i understood the port was ink and the blank air between
us
was an application for citizenship. the words of our fractured speech,
foreign to both him and me, were the answers to write on the thin lines.

towing

a procession of tow trucks
cross the intersection, single file.

a wrecker's body lies inside
the cold, glistening solitude

of a car which never crashes.
time is no essence, now.

caution lights will burn brighter,
            (minute, flashing suns,
            warning against the possibilities)
there being no hooks along the road

to haul away the mess of our impact.
they're dragging humanity this morning.

and that night wagon could roll with abandon,
having so much weight, so close behind,

but he drifts, slowly,
and we notice, slowly.

we sit, running late,
with one foot on the brake,

both hands clutching
our faith in ourselves,

fingers gripping a dark wheel
and notice.

the apocalypse of reason

the apocalypse of reason

I consider the park
and the swings
about us,
an evening breeze
sauntering passed;
a cool ocean caress.

I wonder about those swings, forlorn,
set against a sky which is
bending over and slipping down
a sharp drop
to the   coast.

       it's a simple tale, really with out
       deeper understanding
       really.
       I'm sorry;
       Pray -
       Continue

You turned abruptly
from the muddied path
made soft
from an afternoon shower.
I followed.

You didn't say a word
or hint at
your intentions.

'We were too old to be there.'

I remember telling you
as you squeezed
into the canvas strap
dangling from chains.

We were too old and you smiled
and dangled there.

I find my mind going
through the motions:

my hands
gently meeting your lower back,
as it sailed through the air.
my arms
finding a firmer resistance
as you rose

and I pushed
You away.

> *I can't be quiet,*
> *I don't want you to be misled;*
> *To lose yourself*
> *in your own subtext.*
>
> *This story is not about you.*
> *It is not even about them.*
>
> *It would seem, on the surface,*
> *a story about a girl and a boy;*
> *Woman and man.*
>
> *it is not.*
>
> *It is*
> *man against nature*
> *man against god*
> *man against man*
> *man against himself*
> *man against memory*
> *and how all these things deceive him*
>
> *It is about   things*
> *he'll not tell you.*

The harder I pushed,
the faster you came
back to me.

I see your head bow,

your feet thrust forward,
stretched legs,
your long summer skirt
flirting with the distant trees.

I hear ,
as if the sound was born
in my ears,
your screaming laughter.

He is about to drop
his baggage.
You'll be there
to pick it up and pack it up
in the trunk. start the engines,
let's go for a ride.

He works his chemicals into a frenzy
with a stiff drink.
We're off.

I'm full of warm beer and greasy burgers.
The coffee is cold and strong.

I don't mean to intrude,
but there needs to be guidance.

The fire of his   sunshiny world
may set you to twirling.

Keep an even keel.
There is a deeper meaning
here.
There must be.
We travel this life as
intellectual beasts,
with the keen ability
to reason.

There is always
reason

I can't walk

past
　　　　a park

without these images,
sounds and smells
alongside.

I want to ask you to swing.

I wait for you
to turn
without notice.
I remember
being there,

but I don't remember why.

　　　　My analytic
nature keeps looking
for that reason;
　　　　data,
and because
　　　　it is not there
it tries
　　　　to dismiss
the entire affair

I need you to make
the same decision;

　　　　re:　　　action.
　　　　empirical course .

I need
　　　　to understand

what caused the change.

　　　　Did he mention the sun was setting?
　　　　Did he mention the sharp angle
　　　　creeping under the darker clouds
　　　　of the afternoon rain?　Did he

mention the long shadows Lurking?
High walls restricting light; lurking
shadows crawling slowly to where
he stood; Where he continues to stand?

i thought not.

Be wary,   dark shadows
are moving their forces
to the border,
coming to occupy.
They'll not afford you
the freedom;   the birthright
he would.
                    Shadows lurk.

Lurking

                                        do you hear how
                                        he says good-bye
                                        to your body,
                                        Mother?

                                        do the sounds
                                        of his cries
                                        reverberate
                                        in your spine?

                                        do you quickly
                                        witness the fade
                                        as he stumbles
                                        down a road
                                        not yours?

we've shared
moments;
                    touches;
waves randomly rolling
to the shores of our egos.

when you   decided

to stop.

when the threats of jumping
from a soaring height

over a dangerous distance
had removed themselves
from the bluffs
and you

stopped

when your bare toes dug
into the damp sand,

and you

stopped

within the easy grasp
of my arms,
I felt
as if I had the pounding hearts
of forty warriors in my chest.

I was facing an army of thousands.

> *he can't get*
> *where he wants to go.*
> *he'll never find*
> *that quantum moment*
> *of what he is-*
> > *what he was –*
> > > *what he should be*

> *because he won't look for it.*

> *he trusts his recollection*
> *as if it were the womb.*

quixotic circles
turn a man
against his life
turn a man
against his faith
in finding
a destination
other than the wall

the sun abandoned them

                                    when light was needed.
                               when seeing was paramount,
                                    the sun shut their eyes
                              and pulled the lid of the crypt
                                           firmly shut.

                                        the sun left them
                                               standing
                                 in their chemical imbalance
                                    teetering on the edge
                                         of his demise.

simplicity escapes
through the loop holes
it was born with;

this is simple:

his entire #### was designed
to make him forget.

                                                              everything

she moved her body
in a sway
toward a childhood
abandoned and forlorn.

he followed
because it was easy.

he followed
knowing he would forget.

these memories won't fade

with every passing breath
the strength of my affection
returns me to the moment

when I pushed
and you returned

then I pushed
and you returned

and when I could push
no more
you disembarked
and buried
your *SELF* in my arms
and I buried my **pain**
in your smile.

                                        the face is a graveyard
                                        of uneven depths

         with tombs of dead smiles;
                  passed glances;
   decaying twinkles in the eyes
                       rotting
                 half exposed

    by the holes dug in the field
             by those searching
   for images lost in the battle;
 smells forgotten by weak love;
   touches removed by change

                   the skin
    we held each other against
    has long since been wiped
           from the mantle
              and dusted
      from the chandelier

        we rouse at a wake
    and sweep the floor clean

are you ready
for a happy ending?
we have (clarified) man
and woman
we have man with the memory
of woman

this could be any kind of
connection
so long as there was a

connection
so long as both believe the
connection
so long as you were not a part of
That connection
do not feel
connected

we have a man,
we have a memory
and it is his,
not yours or mine
and we have   a ship

kind of....

we needed   a ship

so like all good clichés
it could pass us in the night
because the night is fast upon us

only he doesn't see it yet

he has ALL his eyes closed.

I see, clearly,
your fisted hand
tightly wrap and bend
the chains;   your body
laid out like a missile;
a rocket;   your
head bent   back

the long auburn locks
tickle the skin of the earth.
HOW it quivered;   HOW
I shivered   -a cool breeze
running through
my thoughts

he doesn't know
auburn, he doesn't
recognize the tricks
a desperate sun plays
as it grabs her hair;
there in front of him

she had it coloured
from the dull brown
of her birth

but let's be fair,
I'll be fair —it's
no concern of yours.

he just doesn't know auburn

moments always
pass

a procession
of the holy, candle-handed
moan and chant,
circling his cathedral.

she keeps his belief
like a ransom note.

he walked away
from all the choices
your pain provided him,
mother.

were your eyes
closed
when your life
was given a freedom
not meant for you?

watch the clock
crawl across his skin
like a louse.

When we walk
the streets
where you can wrap me up;
where I can lose myself
in the course of you,

I rub my hands
in anticipation
of being the support
against your falling backward.

I want to drive you
on
into the **coming night** sunset.

I can feel the heat
of your laugh   *feels, feels....*
wrap me like a **storm** sheet.

I th*ink*
it was the closet
I ever felt to someone.

> *he doesn't know*
> *close.*
> *he doesn't know*
> *anyone.*
> *he doesn't know*
> *ever.*

**did you ever teach him
to be wary
of the thieves lurking
on the crest of night,
mother?**

was there time?

145

Now;
>*now*
we turn together
and pass the park

I can't **resist.**
I ask you;,   trying

to **hide**   the imploring

tied around my tongue
like a **noose,**

'**do you want to swing?**'

>*can you see how the stomach pulled in on him, how the hands were tightly tucked into the pockets, how the left foot just missed the ground and he had to catch himself? can you see how he attempts to run from his errant posture?*
>*there's the bags. there's the kneeling. there's the stuff all happy endings are made of. sing with me…. **you are my sunshine, my only sunshine you make me**….silly, always silly when the senses drip from the hole in the bottom of the … …*

I ask you
and you turn,
to **cross**
the street

"don't be silly,
we're too old
to be doing that."

>he circles his
>memory
>>as a planet.

>the path he chose

                                        always coming back
                                              to you.

the night comes
and goes
and comes
and goes

I circle the block
questioning, wondering,
what it was
which bade me to follow;
which made me feel?
what question was
asked,
knowing
there would be
no answer?

everything comes back

      to the point

when the body, the mind, the soul
were one, covered in flesh
an ocean wrapping us
in its warm arms;
inside a bubble;
without the touch;
no pushing, no coming back

just floating in the potential

awaiting the possibilities

then there was distance
earshot echoes and refusal

you were the lead, I followed
you failed
me
I failed
me
I

i

i

I consider the park
and the swings
about us,
an evening breeze
sauntering passed;
a cool ocean caress.

I wonder about those
swings, forlorn,
set against a sky which is
bending over and slipping down
a sharp drop
to the   coast.

        a simple tale
        how a moment becomes a life

        how a life becomes a memory

        how a memory plays on a swing

masses

swift vessel I: burning

Credo

smoke has unravelled
from the hope of her life,
her shelter from wind and rain
reduced to blackened char,
and i burn against her, still.

what is life is also death.
what soothes can suffocate.
every day another photograph
curls and blisters.
memory is lost in the shadow
cast by passion's pyre

Hymn/Hymen

"Of all base passions fear is most accurs'd."

William Shakespeare; Henry V, Part 1

Philo and Sophia

     39 That which was torn by wild beasts I did not bring to you; I bore the loss of it myself; of my hand you required it, whether stolen by day or stolen by night.   40 Thus I was; by day the heat consumed me, and the cold by night, and my sleep fled from my eyes.

Genesis 31:39-40

swift vessel II: poison

Credo

when eyes become infections,
vision alters with dry words.
under breath, there are demons
which would possess these children:
dreams and faith.

the kettle cannot boil long enough
to rid the blood of anger,
disappointment or pain.
we perfect our skills in deserts,
sniffing sand and drinking the heat;
hunting the scorpion's kiss.

Hymn/Hymen

Alas! they had been friends in youth;
But whispering tongues can poison truth,
And constancy lives in realms above;
And life is thorny, and youth is vain;
And to be wrothe with one we love
Doth work like madness in the brain.

Samuel Coleridge; Christabel

Philo and Sophia

Do horses run upon rocks? Does one plow the sea with oxen? But you
have turned justice into poison and the fruit of righteousness into
wormwood—

Amos 6: 12

swift vessel III: volatile love

Credo

the pressure beneath our skin.
the thin wafer between solid and molten.
we are set to burst, to rise
against the innocent air, as villains,
to hurl our birth into the darkness.

the storm's cohorts,
the wind, the cloud and the rain
separate each other's worth
and so do we;
dividing skin and blood
in a squall toward breathing.

Hymn/Hymen

For I am a weed,
Flung from the rock, on
Ocean's foam, to sail,
Where'er the surge may sweep,
the tempest's breath prevail.

Lord Byron; Childe Harold (canto III)

Philo and Sophia

28 A perverse man spreads strife, and a whisperer separates close friends.

Proverbs 16:28

swift vessel IV: grave

Credo

we have become pinned
to each other, to the floor,
to the hardened silence;
eternally held against
our will, our protest.

the ground will not release us.
the grinding will not abate.
the hole in our philosophy
is dark, damp and final.
we are serving a life sentence
for crimes of wisdom, and of love.

Hymn/Hymen

Such harmony is in immortal souls;
But whilst this muddy vesture of decay
Doth grossly close it in, we cannot hear it

William Shakespeare; The Merchant of Venice, Act V,
Sc 1

Philo and Sophia

25 Make friends quickly with your accuser,
while you are going with him to court,
lest your accuser hand you over to the judge,
and the judge to the guard, and you be put in prison;
26 truly, I say to you, you will never get out
till you have paid the last penny.

Matthew 5: 25-26

swift vessel V: addendum, light's cold reflection

Credo

her face is the mirror;
a scratched quicksilver
exposing only age;
a book of images,
quickly understood and then shut.

she will not lie
about her emptiness
or her trust in others
to give her value,
to give her life. her meaning
is wrapped in dark blankets.

Hymn/Hymen

So little distant dangers seem:
So we mistake the future's face,
Ey'd thro' Hope's deluding glass;
As yon summits soft and fair,
Clad in colours of the air,
Which to those who journey near,
Barren, brown, and rough appear.

John Dyer; Grongar Hill

Philo and Sophia

     23 For if any one is a hearer of the word and not a doer, he is
like a man who observes his natural face in a mirror;
     24 for he observes himself and goes away and at once forgets
what he was like.

James 1: 23-24

.

swift vessel VI: hostility

Credo

love should be red?
when did this quaking silence
gather the strength to move bodies
further from thought
than i am, now, from you?

all things rage:
oceans, wind, rain,
passion, loins, hunger.
every touch is an attack,
be it to conquer flesh
or to conquer the distance.

Hymn/Hymen

Night comes, world-jewelled, . . .
The stars rush forth in myriads as to wage
War with the lines of
Darkness; and the moon,
Pale ghost of
Night, comes haunting the cold earth
After the sun's red sea-death—quiet less.

Phillip James Bailey; Festus

Philo and Sophia

     9 If a wise man has an argument with a fool,
the fool only rages and laughs, and there is no quiet.

Proverbs 29: 9

swift vessel VII: intangible beast

Credo

the hard truth rips through
the spirit of our intentions.
meaning is a menacing force,
haunting all matter,
from the spoon to the nail.

i would hold out my hand,
stretched toward the beast,
fingers unafraid.
the size of its belly, its hunger,
insignificant
beside the looming idea of my need.

Hymn/Hymen

I look for ghosts; but none will force
Their way to me; 'tis falsely said
That even there was intercourse
Between the living and the dead.

William Wordsworth; Affliction of Margaret

Philo and Sophia

18 For you have not come to what may be touched,
 a blazing fire, and darkness, and gloom, and a tempest,
19 and the sound of a trumpet, and a voice whose words
made the hearers entreat that no further messages be spoken to them.

Hebrews 12: 18-19

swift vessel VIII: adornment

Credo

the threads around your neck,
be them hide or gold,
frame your harvest;
the yield bending my spine,
sinking me further in mud.

would i be convicted,
chancing a morsel of your bounty,
hiding a taste of your fertile land
beneath my tattered cloak
or would you hang me
in a gentler noose of arms?

Hymn/Hymen

Just as the felon condemn'd to die—
With a very natural loathing—
Leaving the sheriff to dream of ropes,
From his gloomy cell in a vision elopes,
To caper on sunny greens and slopes,
Instead of the dance upon nothing.

Thomas Hood; Miss Kilmansegg and Her Precious Leg

Philo and Sophia

10 Thou waterest its furrows abundantly,
settling its ridges, softening it with showers,
and blessing its growth.
11 Thou crownest the year with thy bounty;
the tracks of thy chariot drip with fatness.
12 The pastures of the wilderness drip,
the hills gird themselves with joy,
13 The meadows clothe themselves with flocks,
the valleys deck themselves with grain,
they shout and sing together for joy.
Psalm 65: 10-13

swift vessel IX: exposure

Credo

he's twisting against expectation-
rolling his lot toward the edge-
a crushing impact landing
on his blind side, his heart-
laid down without consent.

when the walls are levelled,
that horn's blast a decisive song,
everything built of assumption,
-of hoping, -of believing,
becomes fuel for the enemies fire;
-trinkets, -worthless, -sentimental.

Hymn/Hymen

You'll see that, since our fate is ruled by chance,
Each man, unknowing, great,
Should frame life so that at some future hour
Fact and his dreamings meet.

Victor Hugo; To His Orphan Grandchildren

Philo and Sophia

25 And they waited till they were utterly at a loss;
but when he still did not open the doors of the roof chamber,
they took the key and opened them;
and there lay their lord dead on the floor.

Judges 3: 25

swift vessel X: depth

Credo

who has drowned themselves
in the salty waters of longing?
who has refused to surface
from the depth of love's pain?
who plays suffering's game?

there is too much romance
in anguish,
yet no one cleaning the filth.
i am tired of living beneath dirt;
of never having a clean cup,
filled with cool, fresh water.

Hymn/Hymen

The image of Eternity--the throne
Of the Invisible; even from out thy slime
The monsters of the deep are made; each zone
Obeys thee; thou goest forth, dread, fathomless, alone.

Lord Byron; Childe Harold, Canto IV

Philo and Sophia

7 Many waters cannot quench love,
neither can floods drown it.
If a man offered for love
all the wealth of his house,
it would be utterly scorned.

Solomon 8: 7

swift vessel XI: outcast

Credo

would we be unique bodies still
if we grew entwined,
never having space to stretch opinions;
to bring the thread lacing us to its very end?

we spin, endless, in darkness,
alone, always,
at a governed distance,
across a floor of emptiness.

all those bodies, dripping
with the liquids of life,
in an orgy of simplicity,
in the passionate grip of being.

heavenly bodies,
drifting, dancing, spinning;
never knowing the harm, the thrill
of getting too close;
mixing rocky flesh and flesh.

when definitions were inflexible
i was such a body.
i knew loyalty.
i knew predictability.
i knew you, all of you.

my distance became a crime;
my peers, arrogant;
and my youth a liability.
i was made to understand
stature and seniority.

i am left wandering this icy horde,
lost with the nameless,
left remembering a time
when someone knew what to call me.

i've become the empty plate.
i'm neither ghost nor gravestone.
no water for thirst.
no salt for tears.

here, at the furthest distance
from your warmth,
from the light of your joy,
i'm cast out,
becoming the dry well;
the missing verse.

pray for me, as i wander.
sing for me, as i dance.
laugh for me, as i suffer.
burn for me, as i freeze.
i am not so far as your memory,
nor as broken as your sky.

Hymn/Hymen

What exile from himself can flee?
To zones, though more and more remote,
Still, still pursues, where'er I be,
The blight of life--the demon Thought.

Lord Byron; Childe Harold, To Inez (canto I)

Philo and Sophia

7 its mistress is stripped,
she is carried off,
her maidens lamenting,
moaning like doves,
and beating their breasts.

Nahum 2: 7

Acknowledgements

i would like to thank the following for their support in putting this collection together:

Dale Winslow and Steve Szewczok for the many years of bouncing work back and forth as our informal group "?=!" .

also, i want to thank the great team that is NeoPoiesis Press, for their effort in the creation of this volume!

i'd be remiss if i didn't mention the fantastic writers and readers of the "Myspace" years, whose talent and friendship inspired me to write many of these pieces, including the best reader of all Tami St. Germaine and writers Amanda Joy, Gillian, Frank Axworthy, Petra Whitely, and a woman i know only as 'sometimes sarah' from ontario, whose powerful words were delivered like blows from a warrior, where ever she is. there are too many more to mention here.

i would also like to thank my brother Paul, who, when i was young, read a poem i wrote and said it was good. positive encouragement of the young cannot be underestimated.

finally, i'd like to lUvingly thank Lizete, my wife and closest friend, for her understanding and belief in me, no matter how much my lack of confidence frustrated her.

About the Author

william marshe is an Island son of Cape Breton, on Canada's east coast. He spent his early years immersed in a vibrant culture of artists, writers, singers and thespians, where he wrote, directed, acted in and designed many productions. Like many of the youth of the economically challenged area of Sydney, he left his home as a young adult to seek gainful employment elsewhere and now resides in Toronto, Ontario, working as a millwork designer for luxury homes, locally and around the globe. He continues to write when every moment presents itself.

salt/ /water is william's first collection of poetry. His work has appeared online and in the journal *ETC,* as well as in the collection *The Medium is The Muse [Channeling Marshall McLuhan]* published by NeoPoiesis Press.

NeoPoiesis: *a new way of making*

1) in ancient Greece, poiesis referred to the process of making: creation - production - organization - formation - causation

2) a process that can be physical and spiritual, biological and intellectual, artistic and technological, material and teleological, efficient and formal

3) a means of modifying the environment and a method of organizing the self, the making of art and music and poetry, the fashioning of memory and history and philosophy, the construction of perception and expression and reality

4) an independent publisher with a steadfast goal to print and promote outstanding poets, writers and artists that reflect the creative drive and spirit of the new electronic landscape

NeoPoiesisPress.com

www.ingramcontent.com/pod-product-compliance
Lightning Source LLC
Chambersburg PA
CBHW021104090426
42738CB00006B/501